LAUNCH AN ATTACK

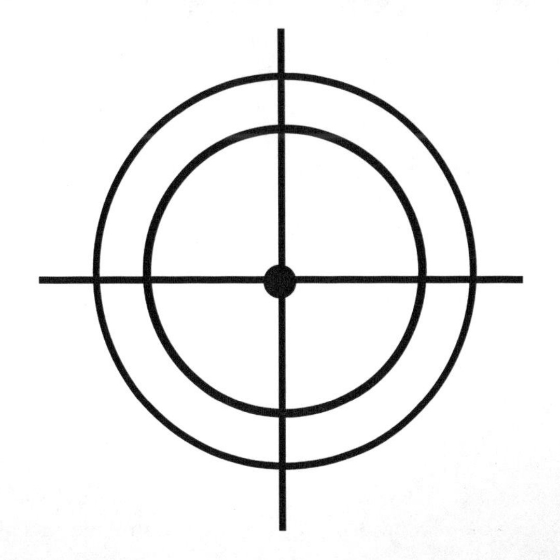

Ayana Prudhomme

WestBow Press books may be ordered through booksellers or by contacting:

WestBow Press
A Division of Thomas Nelson & Zondervan
1663 Liberty Drive
Bloomington, IN 47403
www.westbowpress.com
1 (866) 928-1240

ISBN: 978-1-4908-3142-8 (sc)
ISBN: 978-1-4908-3141-1 (e)

Library of Congress Control Number: 2014905475

Printed in the United States of America.

WestBow Press rev. date: 05/19/2014

Dedication

To the first gifts given to me by God; my parents Margaret Joseph and Ronald Nurse- I honor You

Table of Contents

Psalm 119-105: Thy word is a lamp unto my feet and a light unto my path

PSALM

Oh Lord, my God, how excellent is Your Name in all the earth!
When I consider thy ways and thy loving-kindness toward me
Oh how marvellous are you!
When I think about the gifts You have given me
How awesome is Your Name!
When I think about the time You have spent with me
How glorious is Your Presence!
When I think of the fact that You live in me
How mighty are Your hands!
When I think of what Your hands have made for me
How endless is Your ability!
When I think about the trials You've brought me through
How magnificent is Your power!
When I think of the blessings You've bestowed upon me
How great is Your love!
When I think about what You've done for me
How sufficient is Your mercy!
When I think about the authority You've given me
How perfect is Your grace!
When I think of the sacrifice You've made for me
How powerful is the Blood!
Oh Lord, my God, how excellent is Your name in all the earth
How great is my God and greatly to be praised!

BOW

Don't tell me I'm ill and try to fool my body;
Spirit of affliction, BOW!
Don't tell me to go against my Father's instruction;
Spirit of rebellion, BOW!
Don't tell me how and where to spend my money;
Spirit of poverty, BOW!
Don't try to take the peace from my heart;
Spirit of confusion, BOW!
Don't put my focus on the body and sex;
Spirit of perversion, BOW!
Don't show me my past and all I've done wrong;
Spirit of condemnation, BOW!
Don't tell me I can't and I'm not strong;
Spirit of fear, BOW!
Don't tell me I'm not loved, I'm not good enough;
Spirit of rejection, BOW!
Don't tell me I can't shout, clap and dance;
Spirit of religion, BOW!

I know who I am, I'm saved by grace
I'll let you know this face to face
I'm filled with the Spirit and washed in the Blood
A banner is lifted when You come in as a flood
I'm an heir to the kingdom
I've authority and dominion
So I stand with boldness and declare right now
"Satan! The Blood of Jesus is against you and you have to BOW!"

VICTORY

I have the keys to victory, and one of them is praise;
No matter what you're going through just let your voices raise
Another key to victory, is the mighty Word of God,
So stand up and declare, the double-edged sword
This special key to victory is just a little faith,
Keep on hoping and believing, you're miracle's not late
A mighty key to victory is that of prayer and fast,
The blessing you've been waiting on is sure to come at last
A final key to victory is in His name and Blood
You call this Name at anytime; He comes in as a flood
So the special door to victory; belongs to you and me
We simply need to walk with Him and use the victory keys

IT'S THAT SIMPLE

Building a relationship is what I need to do
To talk to You and look to You in good and bad times too
To recognize You for who You are and say thanks for what You've done
To tell others of your greatness and of Jesus Christ your Son
You lead me with your sceptre, now all belongs to me
Though the arrows point at me, I have the victory
"Want what she's got..." that's the cry of the people
Repent, confess, accept His Son "Yes, it is that simple!"

WHAT I SEE

The troubles, the war, the problems; are all invisible to me
My eyes are overwhelmed with His awesome majesty
The hurt, the pain, the tears, are of no concern to me
I'm blinded only by His magnificent glory
No money, more bills, no food; things I cannot focus on
My eyes are focussed on Him, I'm a part of His kingdom
So when you see me smiling, through all of life's rough storms
It's not my might, nor my power but what He's overcome
Every time I look around, this is all I see
His grace, His love, His faithfulness and what He means to me

THE ROCK

My Rock is my foundation
It's immovable and never shaken
My Rock is strong and stable
To hold the heaviest weight, it's more than able
My Rock can take the storms of life;
All trials, all pain, all toils and strife
On my Rock I place all that I own
I know it's safe and I'm never alone
My Rock is there when no one's around
To cry on, laugh on or sing a quiet song
On my Rock is where I lay my head
It allows me to have hope when the situation seems dead
Without my Rock I can do nothing
I love my Rock and owe It my everything

ALL ABOUT YOU

They see me strong and wealthy
They watch me with hearts of jealousy
It has nothing to do with me!

Never sick a day
Prospering in all my ways
Blessings without delay
It has nothing to do with me!

My business has doubled twice
Great joy in family life
Full of peace and no more strife
It has nothing to do with me!

Pressure and worries are gone
My greatest battles I've won
The map of my future is drawn
It has nothing to do with me!

People watch me and say
"For whatever she's got I'll pay"
But what I've got is free
'Cause Jesus died for me
He gives me liberty
And sets the captives free

So when you look at me
As I be all I can be
The one thing that I've done
Is receive Jesus Christ God's Son

Mark 11:24- Therefore I tell you, whatever you ask for in prayer, believe that you have received it and it will be yours. (ESV)

MY FUTURE

I look into my future and this is what I see
Health, peace and prosperity
Problems and trials coming from left to right
I see I'm victorious in this great fight

My children are grown and full of success
They're practicing love and won't settle for less
My husband has gotten wrinkles by his eyes
Yet he's so handsome, strong and wise

The world all around has changed oh so vast
It resembles nothing of my precious past
Though it seems gloomy, helpless and dread
I choose to look at its beauty instead
My strength and body's not what is used to be
But I'm blessed, at peace and extremely happy
The sacrifices I'm making each night in prayer
Seems to have paid off and my future in clear

I'm glad I've allowed Him to always lead me
For my future seems secure, full of joy and mercy
By faith I stretch towards the Prize
For I'm the apple of my Father's eyes!

COMPLAINING?

I'm tired of struggling; from the pain I'm sore
Can somebody tell me what all this fighting's for?
Suddenly I heard a voice; so soft, yet plain
"There you go; complaining again!
When times are great you love Me so
If it's not your way, to hell I go.
I shelter and clothe you, give you food to eat,
Always making sure you don't stumble at your feet
The sun in the sky is just for you
The clouds, the trees, the waters too
I keep my eyes on you all day long,
I even send the birds to sing you a song
The opportunities I present are unmentionable
You have your job, your health, and you're mentally stable
You hurt Me. You always turn your back on Me
Yet still, I can't help but love you unconditionally
I want to know what you're complaining about,
With every breath that comes out of your mouth
Stop right now, look around for a while
And see all the things I've made to see you smile"

MY HEART'S CRY

I want to spend my life with You Jesus
All day, every season too
In my heart, my mind, my soul, all of my being
That's where I want You to be
My every thought screams for Jesus
My heart longs for Jesus
Your Presence is worth everything to me
I give up all possessions, accomplishments, problems, friends,
family, all earthly possessions, even my life
For Your Presence Jesus
I want You and only You
You are my heart's desire
The desire and longing of my soul is Jesus
My mind yearns to be filled with You
I don't want anything or anyone but You Jesus; to saturate my very being
Pour Yourself on me
Flow through me
Be with me
Always........

JESUS IS....

My Joy
My Saviour
My Lover
My Peace
My Strength
My Healer
My Father
My Provider
My Source
My Comfort
My Restorer
My Deliverer
My God
My Protector
My Redeemer
My Shelter
My Miracle Worker
My Rock
My Teacher
My Helper
My Blessing
My Treasure
My Grace
My Prized Possession
My Reward

My Trophy of Excellence
Faithful
Dependable
Truth
Life
Good
Perfect
Mighty
Majesty
King
Holy
A Friend
A Brother
Exemplar
Just
Righteous
Lovely
Trustworthy
Patient
Kind
Powerful
Gentle
Strong
Humble
A Leader
Compassionate
Jesus is EVERYTHING I NEED and so much more!!!!!

I SEE JESUS

I see Jesus when:
Bills are due
Sickness comes
Storms arise
Depression creeps in
Friends disappoint
My heart is broken
Temptation is present
Persecution hits
I need a friend
I've done my all
I'm blinded
Confusion starts
All else fails
I'm all alone
Trouble's all around

No matter what comes...I see Jesus!
My eyes are fixed
On You Jesus!

PRAISE THE LORD!

Praise the Lord;
He saves me
He loves me
He heals me
He provides for me
He protects me
He comforts me
He delivers me
He blesses me
He serves me
He honours me
He satisfies me
He embraces me
He convicts me
He disciplines me
He instructs me

He guides me
He moves me
He transforms me
He calls me
He favours me
He forgives me
He redeems me
He helps me
He knows me
He amazes me
He cleanses me
He keeps me
He separates me
He promotes me
He pleases me
He sees me

WHO AM I?

I die daily
I decrease
I surrender
I stand still
I yield fully
I cast all cares
I rest
I am nothing but for Christ Who lives in me.

Isaiah 41:10

fear not, for I am with you; be not dismayed, for I am your God; I will strengthen you, I will help you, I will uphold you with my righteous right hand.

WHAT ABOUT ME?!

I lied
I sold my body
I hated
I murdered
I cheated
I raped
I stole
I was addicted
I cursed
I bullied
I abused
I disobeyed
I blasphemed
I worshipped idols
I doubted
I sodomised
Why do you look down at me?
He loves me!
Didn't He die for me?
"While we were sinners, Christ died for us!"

STEADFAST

The waves of life pushed me to and fro
But I held on to Your Word

I was broke and depressed
But I held on to Your Word

My life was filled with horror and stress
But I held on to Your word

I was brought to the point of death
But I held on to Your Word

My strength was gone, trouble surrounded me
But I held on to Your word

The enemy's devices tried to cloud me
But I held on to Your word

Hallelujah, I have the victory
'Cause I held on to Your word

TREASURE

I found It!!!
It's worth far more than rubies
No billionaire can ever buy
All the gold in the world
Can't purchase it, don't even try

It's fabulous, more beautiful than words can permit
Too exorbitant and awesome; my mind can hardly contain it
I searched, I looked, I sought high and low
To find this fabulous treasure that causes my heart to glow

Right before my eyes; there all along for me
Was the love of Jesus and it was for free!!!

LOCK DOWN

Temptation came and I resisted
Sin is on lock down!
My body's in pain and I worry not
Sickness is on lock down!
Lost my job and still have a smile
Poverty is on lock down!
Been hurt and abused but still have joy
Unforgiveness is on lock down!
Walking tall with my head up high
Fear is on lock down!
All sadness is gone, I'm full of glee
Depression is on lock down!
Negativity, stress and all darkness is gone
Satan is on lock down!!!

A LOVE SONG

At the mention of Your name, my heart bows in reverence
Because I love You
The sound of Your voice makes me shiver with delight
Because I love You
Everything You made I cherish forever
Because I love You
Your touch makes me weak in the knees
Because I love You
When I'm in Your Presence, it's indescribable
Because I love You
Your words always bring me comfort and peace
Because I love You
My eyes only see visions of You
Because I love You
When I think about You and all we've been through, I want You to know
I will always love You

JESUS YOU

Jesus You, fill me with Your love
To You, I offer all my praise
Lord You are, Lord above all Lords
It's all about You Jesus

Jesus You are, the King of above all kings
You're, the Bright and Morning Star
Jesus; Forgiver of my sins
You are Great, oh so great!

Jesus, what a wonder You are
Sweet Jesus, Mighty King and Ruler
My Jesus, the Alpha and Omega
Sweet Jesus, come Jesus

THANK YOU

Thank You for the cross
Thank You for restoring everything I'd lost
Thank You for Your love
Thank you for Your blessings from above
Thank You for Your touch
Thank You for loving me so much

Thank You for Your peace
Thank You that the strife has ceased
Thank You for providing for me
Thank You for Your tender mercy

Thank You for abundant grace
Thank You that I can see You face to face
Thank You for Your healing power
Thank you for being my Saviour

There are so many things I want to thank You for
Thank You that I'm your beloved; whom You truly adore!

Romans 8:37

No, in all these things we are more than conquerors through Him who loves us (ESV)

PASSION

You were beaten, You bled, You died for me
To keep me free from sickness, death and poverty
You were mocked, humiliated, treated unfairly
For me to become royalty

Dragged, laughed at, made a mockery of
So that I can receive Your matchless love
Guiltless, blameless, full of purity
No one has ever shown such love for me
You proved Your love at Calvary
And showed how far You'll go for me

GUARANTEED

There is one true guarantee:

- To peace
- To prosperity
- To joy
- Hope
- Love
- Redemption
- Miracles
- Healing
- Deliverance
- Success
- Victory
- Unmerited favour
- Blessing

HIS NAME IS JESUS!!!

HOLY SPIRIT

You talk with me, show me the way
Guide my footsteps each and everyday
Fill me with power no other can show
Enable me to get up and go

Strengthen me when life is tough
Lift my burdens, free me from unnecessary stuff
Give my lips the right words to say
Comfort me so I know I'll be okay

Empower me so I can teach
Give me passion so the lost I can reach
You bless me with wisdom so I can give
Satisfy me with healthy; long life I will live

Charge me with influence and favour
To You alone will my soul surrender

YOU ARE THERE

Although life's challenges surround me
I know You are there
When everyone seems against me
I know You are there
Sickness tried to kill me
I know You are there
Financial struggles overwhelm me
I know You are there
Children rebel against me
I know You are there
Friends came to deceive me
I know You are there
Family tries to accuse me
I know You are there
Co workers want to use me
I know You are there
They all would have defeated me
Had I not known; Jesus You are there!

ANOINTED WORDS

I declare:
By His stripes I am healed
I am the head and not the tail
No weapon formed against me prospers
All of my needs are met
With long life God satisfies me
He provides everything for my enjoyment
As for me and my household we serve the Lord
Goodness and mercy follow me all the days of life
Be it unto me, oh Lord according to Your word
(Taken from the Holy Word)

NOW

This is Your time Lord to be glorified
This is Your time to be magnified
Shine Jesus shine; let Your Light be seen

This is Your time to be revealed
Manifest Yourself in all Your glory
Shine Jesus shine; let Your Light be seen

Perfect Yourself in me
Show us Your majesty
Fulfil my destiny
Shine Jesus shine, let Your Light be seen

Ignite Your favour Lord
So that I may move forward
Shine Jesus shine; let Your Light be seen

This is Your time of honour
Make Your Name known forever
Shine Jesus shine; let Your Light be seen

WHERE I BELONG

I belong in Your Presence
I belong in Your word
I belong in Your wisdom
I belong in Your strength
I belong in Your revelation
I belong in Your purpose
I belong in Your peace
I belong in Your love
I belong in You Jesus

Jeremiah 29:11

For I know the plans I have for you, declares the Lord, plans for welfare and not for evil, to give you a future and a hope

EXAMPLE

I arrive; the atmosphere shifts
I command; it is established
I touch; they are healed
I sow; I reap in abundance
I bind; it halts
I loose; it's released
I bless; it multiplies
I speak; lives are transformed
I believe; it is done
I agree; it is delivered
As Jesus did, so do I and much more!

STEPPING OUT

You placed an uncommon seed in me
Told me exactly what it should be
I'm stepping out in faith

Don't know how to start but won't worry
Expecting Your Spirit to guide me
I'm stepping out in faith

Declaring favour as I plan to see
This seed blossom into a tree
I'm stepping out in faith

Knowing Your hand is upon me
This dream is now reality
I'm stepping out in faith

Thank You for the money, the influence, the opportunity
Thank You for the honour; to Your Name I give all glory

HUNGRY

I need to know You intimately
Without Your Presence I'm empty
I'm seeking daily to behold Your majesty
My soul is hungry

Nothing can satisfy this longing but You
I'm stretching and reaching to touch the heart of You
You are King, Father, Almighty
My soul is hungry

Satisfy my soul, Oh Lord
Quench this thirst
Consume me with Your glory
My soul is hungry

SHHH!

Life's so busy, hustling up and down
Silence! I need to hear...
My heart is racing; so many things to do
Silence! I need to hear...
Distracted mind; problems and toils
Silence! I need to hear...
Complaints, regrets, losing direction
Silence! I need to hear...
It's overwhelming; discouragement, I seem to be lost
Silence! I need to hear...
Bad news, destruction, chaos all around
Silence! I need to hear...

IN MY HEART

In my heart I hold Your law
In my heart I keep Your peace
In my heart Your promises are written
It's all in my heart

In my heart is Your will
In my heart I trust and obey
In my heart I thirst for You
It's all in my heart

In my heart is Your righteousness
In my heart I receive Your grace
In my heart I keep Your truth
It's all in my heart

BLESSED

I'm blessed- His hands are on me
I'm blessed- I walk in the counsel of the godly
I'm blessed- I dwell in safety
Boy, am I blessed!

I'm blessed- He considers my sighing
I'm blessed- His love is unfailing
I'm blessed- He has heard my weeping
Boy, am I blessed!

I'm blessed- In me He takes pleasure
I'm blessed- I'm free from danger
I'm blessed- He watches me forever
Boy, am I blessed

I'm blessed- I'm never forsaken
I'm blessed- My spirit He awakens
I'm blessed- His purpose's not hidden
Boy, am I blessed

DELIVERANCE

He delivers me in times of trouble
And pays me back double for my trouble
He delivers me from the hands of my enemy
He delivers me from death and poverty

He delivers me from the bed of affliction
He delivers me from shame and temptation
He delivers me from vicious lying tongues
He delivers me from holds that were too strong

He delivers me from a shameful past
He delivers my soul that was downcast
He delivers me from being a reproach to my neighbour
He delivers me I'm free now and forever

Acknowledgments

To my husband Sheldon Prudhomme; your love and support is
immeasurable. Thank you for being my number one supporter
To my son Judah Prudhomme; You inspire me to be a better woman everyday
To my Lord and Saviour Jesus Christ; all honour and glory
be unto Your Name! You are my Everything!

Psalm 9:1-2
I will praise you, O LORD, with all
my heart; I will tell of all your
wonders.
I will be glad and rejoice
in you; I will sing praise to your
name, O Most High.

Invitation

That if you confess with your mouth, "Jesus is Lord," and believe in your heart that God raised him from the dead, you will be saved. For it is with your heart that you believe and are justified, and it is with your mouth that you confess and are saved

Romans 10:9-10

I invite you dear reader, to accept Jesus Christ as your Lord and Savior, your life will never be the same!

Please say this prayer:

Lord Jesus, please forgive me of my sins and cleanse me of all unrighteousness. I believe in my heart and confess with my mouth that You died on the cross for my sins and to reconcile me with my heavenly Father. I ask you to come into my heart today, save my soul, make me a new creation. I receive You today. I am saved. Amen

If you have said that prayer, you are now saved and I welcome you into the kingdom of God! Please email me at ayana_prudhomme@yahoo.com and let me know of your decision. Follow me on Twitter at mrsprudz

Printed in the United States
By Bookmasters